Seventies

The Fun Years!

Jim Chumley

summersdale

SEVENTIES: THE FUN YEARS!

Illustrations by John Lightbourne

Summersdale Publishers Ltd
46 West Street
Chichester
West Sussex
PO19 1RP
UK

www.summersdale.com

Printed and bound in China

ISBN: 978-1-84953-116-0

Substantial discounts on bulk quantities of Summersdale books are available to corporations, professional associations and other organisations. For details contact Summersdale Publishers by telephone: +44 (0) 1243 771107, fax: +44 (0) 1243 786300 or email: nicky@summersdale.com.

To...

From...

Being seventy is no different from being sixty-nine. It's a round number, and there's something about roundness that has always appealed.

Elizabeth Taylor

One of the advantages of being seventy is that you need only four hours' sleep. True, you need it four times a day, but still.

Denis Norden

I can still enjoy sex at seventy-four. I live at seventy-five, so it's no distance.

Bob Monkhouse

We grow neither better nor worse as we get old, but more like ourselves.

May L. Becker

Age is just a number. It's totally irrelevant unless, of course, you happen to be a bottle of wine.

Joan Collins

Perhaps one has to be very old before one learns to be amused rather than shocked.

Pearl S. Buck

Please keep
off the grass

Age should not have its face lifted,
but it should rather teach the world to
admire wrinkles as the etchings
of experience.

Ralph B. Perry

I will never give in to old age until I become old. And I'm not old yet!

Tina Turner

You don't get older, you get better.

Shirley Bassey

To be seventy years young is sometimes far more cheerful and hopeful than to be forty years old.

Oliver Wendell Holmes Jr

The older I get the better I used to be.

Lee Trevino

Beautiful young people are accidents
of nature, but beautiful old people are
works of art.

Eleanor Roosevelt

I'm so wrinkled I can screw my hat on.

Phyllis Diller

It is obscene to think that some day
one will look like an old map
of France.

Brigitte Bardot

I'm growing old; I delight in the past.

Henri Matisse

I don't feel old. I don't
feel anything till noon.
That's when it's time for
my nap.

Bob Hope

No man loves life like him that's
growing old.

Sophocles

I don't want my wrinkles taken away —
I don't want to look like everyone else.

Jane Fonda

Good cheekbones are the brassiere
of old age.

Barbara de Portago

The easiest way to diminish the appearance of wrinkles is to keep your glasses off when you look in the mirror.

Joan Rivers

Pleas'd to look forward, pleas'd to look behind, and count each birthday with a grateful mind.

Alexander Pope

I don't want to achieve immortality
through my work... I want to achieve
it through not dying.

Woody Allen

I am prepared to meet my Maker.
Whether my Maker is prepared for…
meeting me is another matter.

Winston Churchill on the eve of his
seventy-fifth birthday

I'm too old to do things by half.

Lou Reed

When they tell me I'm too old to do something, I attempt it immediately.

Pablo Picasso

No woman should ever be
quite accurate about her
age. It looks so calculating.

Oscar Wilde

I do wish I could tell you my age but it's
impossible. It keeps changing
all the time.

Greer Garson

It's not all bad, this getting old, ripening. God forbid I should live long enough to ferment.

Emily Carr

To be seventy years old is like climbing the Alps. You reach a snow-crowned summit, and see behind you the deep valley stretching miles...

Henry Wadsworth Longfellow

The great thing about getting older is
that you don't lose all the other ages
you've been.

Madeleine L'Engle

You'll lose your mind when you grow older. What they don't tell you is that you won't miss it.

Malcolm Cowley

It's great to have grey hair. Ask anyone who's bald.

Rodney Dangerfield

Laughter doesn't require teeth.

Bill Newton

As you grow older, you learn to understand life a little better.

Solomon Burke

If you survive long enough, you're revered – rather like an old building.

Katherine Hepburn

An archaeologist is the best husband a woman can have because the older she gets the more interested he becomes.

Agatha Christie

I am not afraid of ageing, but more afraid of people's reactions to my ageing.

Barbara Hershey

Age is opportunity no less than
youth itself.

Henry Wadsworth Longfellow

Everything you see I owe to spaghetti.

Sophia Loren

As we grow old, the
beauty steals inward.

Ralph Waldo Emerson

Old age is like flying through a storm.
Once you're aboard, there's nothing
you can do.

Golda Meir

Old age isn't so bad when you consider the alternative.

Maurice Chevalier

I'm at an age when my back goes out more than I do.

Phyllis Diller

Age seldom arrives smoothly or quickly. It's more often a succession of jerks.

Jean Rhys

I am like a snowball – the further I am
rolled the more I gain.

Susan B. Anthony

Do not worry about avoiding temptation. As you grow older it will avoid you.

Joey Adams

Inside every older person is a younger
person wondering what the
hell happened.

Cora Harvey Armstrong

I can still cut the mustard… I just
need help opening the jar!

Anonymous

When grace is joined with wrinkles, it is adorable. There is an unspeakable dawn in happy old age.

Victor Hugo

I delight in men over seventy. They always offer one the devotion of a lifetime.

Oscar Wilde

Oh, to be seventy again.

Georges Clemenceau on
seeing a pretty girl on his
eightieth birthday

For all the advances in medicine, there is
still no cure for the common birthday.

John Glenn

I have achieved my seventy years in the usual way… a scheme of life which would kill anybody else.

Mark Twain at his seventieth birthday dinner

Age does not matter if the matter
does not age.

Carlos Peña Romulo

The excess of our youth are cheques
written against our age and they are
payable with interest thirty years later.

Charles Caleb Colton

When you get to my age life seems little more than one long march to and from the lavatory.

John Mortimer

None are so old as those who have
outlived enthusiasm.

Henry David Thoreau

I want to live to be eighty so I can piss more people off.

Charles Bukowski

I love everything that's old: old friends, old times, old manners, old books, old wines.

Oliver Goldsmith

You can't turn back the clock. But you can wind it up again.

Bonnie Prudden

Like everyone else who makes the mistake of getting older, I begin each day with coffee and obituaries.

Bill Cosby

More than anything else, I'd like to be an old man with a good face, like Hitchcock or Picasso.

Sean Connery

A healthy old fellow, who is not a fool,
is the happiest creature living.

Richard Steele

Old people aren't exempt from having
fun and dancing... and playing.

Liz Smith

With mirth and laughter let old
wrinkles come.

William Shakespeare

You can't help getting
older, but you don't have
to get old.

George Burns

If I had my life to live over again, I'd
make the same mistakes, only sooner.

Tallulah Bankhead

If you want a thing done well, get a couple of old broads to do it.

Bette Davis

I have bursts of being a lady, but it
doesn't last long.

Shelley Winters

I didn't get old on purpose, it just happened. If you're lucky, it could happen to you.

Andy Rooney

We thought we were running away from the grown-ups, and now we are the grown-ups.

Margaret Atwood

Some day you will be
old enough to start
reading fairy tales again.

C. S. Lewis

That's something I think is growing on
me as I get older: happy endings.

Alice Munro

A man knows when he is growing old
because he begins to look like
his father.

Gabriel García Márquez

The minute a man ceases to grow, no matter what his years, that minute he begins to be old.

William James

The older I get, the more I realise that just keeping on keeping on is what life's all about.

Janis Ian

Age is not measured by years. Some people are born old and tired while others are going strong at seventy.

Dorothy Thompson

The years teach much
which the days
never knew.

Ralph Waldo Emerson

The longer I live the more beautiful
life becomes.

Frank Lloyd Wright

At my age getting a second doctor's
opinion is kinda like switching
slot machines.

Jimmy Carter

The secret of staying young is to live honestly, eat slowly, and lie about your age.

Lucille Ball

I'm not interested in age.
People who tell me their
age are silly. You're as
old as you feel.

Elizabeth Arden

The ageing process has you firmly in its
grasp if you never get the urge to
throw a snowball.

Doug Larson

You really haven't changed in seventy years. Your body changes… you don't change at all.

Doris Lessing

No matter what happens, I'm loud, noisy, earthy and ready for much more living.

Elizabeth Taylor

Old age is an excellent time for outrage. My goal is to say or do at least one outrageous thing every week.

Maggie Kuhn

www.summersdale.com